NEW VANGUARD 232

THE IMPERIAL JAPANESE NAVY OF THE RUSSO-JAPANESE WAR

MARK STILLE   ILLUSTRATED BY PAUL WRIGHT

First published in Great Britain in 2016 by Osprey Publishing,
PO Box 883, Oxford, OX1 9PL, UK
PO Box 3985, New York, NY 10185-3985, USA
E-mail: info@ospreypublishing.com

Osprey Publishing, part of Bloomsbury Publishing Plc

A CIP catalog record for this book is available from the British Library

Print ISBN: 978 1 4728 1119 6
PDF ebook ISBN: 978 1 4728 1120 2
ePub ebook ISBN: 978 1 4728 1121 9

Index by Alan Rutter
Typeset in Sabon and Myriad Pro
Originated by PDQ Media, Bungay, UK
Printed in China through World Print Ltd

16 17 18 19 20   10 9 8 7 6 5 4 3 2 1

Osprey Publishing supports the Woodland Trust, the UK's leading
woodland conservation charity. Between 2014 and 2018 our
donations are being spent on their Centenary Woods project in
the UK.

www.ospreypublishing.com

CONTENTS

THE IMPERIAL JAPANESE NAVY OF THE RUSSO-JAPANESE WAR

INTRODUCTION

The story of the early Imperial Japanese Navy (IJN) is remarkable by any measure. From its uncertain beginnings in 1868, the new navy could claim to be the fourth largest in the world by the start of the Russo-Japanese War. In that war, against seemingly great odds, the IJN decisively destroyed the Russian fleet, gaining its greatest victory. But this victory sowed the seeds for the destruction of the IJN 40 years later against a far more powerful foe.

In the decades prior to the war, the IJN proved adept at building a balanced fleet, selecting the proper technologies and ordering capable ships from foreign builders. It consistently improved these foreign designs and made them better than comparable ships in foreign navies. Most importantly, the Japanese developed a naval strategy which fitted the capabilities of their new fleet and which led them to victory against a larger opponent. This book is not meant to provide a detailed treatment of the naval aspects of the Russo-Japanese War; rather to give enough background on the conflict to put the designs and capabilities of the IJN's ships into proper context.

THE RISE OF THE IJN

In 1868, Japan's existing Tokugawa feudal structure was overthrown. The clans that supported the new Imperial government viewed naval power as essential to the nation's future if it was to survive the encroachment of foreign powers. It took time though to translate this emphasis on maritime issues into a real navy. Through the 1870s and 1880s, the new Imperial Navy was still a coastal defense force with a small rag-tag collection of ships and a non-professional officer corps.

This lack of baggage in terms of existing ships or attitudes was instrumental in paving the road to building an effective maritime force. It allowed the Japanese to readily adopt the best of Western technology and ideas. Inspired leadership was another important factor which was kick-started by the establishment of a naval academy in Tokyo in 1869. In 1888, the academy

The IJN's first modern battleship was *Fuji*, shown here in June 1897 before her formal commissioning. The delivery of this battleship meant that Japan had joined the club of major naval powers. (Yamato Museum)

was moved to Etajima near Hiroshima and featured merit-based entrance and a modern education. Along with a competent officer corps, the enlisted ranks were filled with a mix of volunteers and later draftees, but both exhibited the highest levels of training and morale.

In 1870, the new government made the British Royal Navy the model for the new Imperial Navy. This brought a new level of training to the IJN and concurrently Japan began to order steam-driven warships from British yards. By the early 1890s, the IJN had developed into a small force with a number of fast and powerfully armed warships. However, Japan still did not have the means to afford a conventional battle fleet with expensive battleships.

The IJN's first test came in the Sino-Japanese War of 1894–95. The Japanese felt confident enough that they were willing to risk their new foreign-built navy, purchased at great cost, against a Chinese Navy with twice as many ships and led by two German-built battleships that the Japanese had no counter to. However, the IJN had unseen advantages, mainly its quick-firing guns and the superior training of its crews. On September 17, 1894, the two fleets met in the battle of the Yalu River. In the ensuing mêlée, half of the Chinese ships were sunk and the other half damaged and forced to return to port. No Japanese ships were lost, and only one received serious damage. China eventually sued for peace, marking Japan as the preeminent Asian power.

The IJN's Build-Up

Under the energetic Yamamoto Gombei (no relation to the Yamamoto Isoruku of the Pacific War), who was the driving force behind the IJN's rapid rise between 1895 and 1906, the IJN experienced a decade of rapid growth following the war with China. Concerned about Japan's victory over China, Russia, Germany and France intervened by reversing some of the terms of the Treaty of Shimonoseki between China and Japan. The Japanese were forced to withdraw from the Liaodong Peninsula, which included Port Arthur. This key base was immediately occupied by Russia. Japan responded by signing an alliance with Great Britain in 1902 and embarking on a major naval build-up.

Before the war with China, Japan had ordered its first two battleships from Great Britain to counterbalance the two German-built battleships already in Chinese hands. Now, partly with the indemnity paid by China after the war, the IJN developed its first construction program which called for another four battleships, eight cruisers (four armored and four protected), 23 destroyers, and 63 torpedo boats. This ambitious plan was approved in 1895 and funded the following year; it was planned that the program would take ten years and two stages to complete. In 1897, the plan was revised because of fears that the size of the Russian fleet assigned to the Far East could be larger than earlier believed. To compensate, the four protected cruisers were deleted and replaced by two armored cruisers. This gave the IJN a "Six-Six Fleet" of six modern battleships and six armored cruisers. Extra battleships would have been preferred, but Japan lacked the means to afford more and the introduction of advanced armor allowed armored cruisers to take their place in the battle line.

Preparations for War with Russia

Following Japan's defeat of China in the war of 1894–95, Russia became Japan's primary potential opponent. Russia had overturned Japan's

This excellent starboard beam view of *Yashima* is from May 1898 after the ship arrived in Japan. The ship looks impressive but, like all battleships of her day, was deficient in underwater protection as was shown when she sank after hitting Russian mines in May 1904. (Yamato Museum)

occupation of Port Arthur after the Sino-Japanese War and was seeking to expand its influence in Manchuria and Korea. This directly clashed with Japan's national security objectives, making a conflict all but inevitable. By late 1903, it was obvious to the Japanese that negotiations with the Russians to reach an accommodation in northeast Asia were leading nowhere, so Japan made preparations for war.

The key to defeating Russia was winning the war at sea. Russia had a powerful Pacific Squadron and this force had to be neutralized in order to move the Imperial Army to Korea so that it could occupy Korea and seize Manchuria; only control of the sea lanes between Japan and Korea would make this possible. In preparation for war, the Imperial Navy was brought up to peak readiness. The IJN's main battle force was the Combined Fleet which included all but local defense forces. In December 1903, the Combined Fleet was reactivated and broken down into two fleets. The First Fleet was the battle line with the IJN's six modern battleships and four protected cruisers, whereas the Second Fleet was a faster force designed for independent operations or screening the battle line in a major fleet action. It included the IJN's six armored cruisers and an array of smaller cruisers, destroyers and torpedo boats. Both the First and Second Fleets were broken down into two squadrons and the balance of the IJN was assigned to the Third Fleet, which was comprised mainly of obsolete and obsolescent units suitable only for coastal defense duties, and complemented by other obsolete units and small torpedo boats for local base defense.

Command of the Combined Fleet was given to Admiral Togo Heihachiro. He was considered by many as a surprise choice, but possessed the ability to calmly consider his options and come up with the correct tactical decision. His selection was an inspired one, and he went on to oversee the IJN's victory in the coming conflict and has become a legend in Japan.

The IJN's operations plan for the upcoming conflict was approved in December 1903. The first stage of the war was to secure Korea, so this meant that the IJN's first priority was to protect the movement of the Imperial Army to Korea, rather than to seek an immediate fleet engagement. In the second phase of the war, the IJN would have to neutralize the Russian fleet. This would not be easy, since the entire Russian Navy greatly outnumbered the IJN. Even considering only the ships deployed to the Far East, and these were the best ships in the Russian Navy, the Russians still enjoyed a numerical advantage over the IJN in battleships. The Japanese feared that the remaining bulk of the Russian Navy in the form of the Baltic Fleet would be deployed to the Far East which would magnify the IJN's numerical inferiority. While on an individual ship basis the IJN was superior, the Russian Navy units in the Far East were all modern units less than ten years old and manned by well-trained crews.

Naval Balance in January, 1904

	IJN	Russian Pacific Squadron	
		Port Arthur	**Vladivostok**
First-class Battleships	6	7	0
Second-class Battleship	1	0	0
Third-class Battleship	1	0	0
Armored Cruisers	8	1	3
Protected Cruisers	15 (+2)	5	1
Unprotected Cruisers	4	4	0
Coastal Defense Ships	7	0	0
Gunboats	8	8	0
Destroyers	20 (+3)	25	0
Torpedo Boats	81 (+7)	0	16

(+x) – indicates the number of ships under construction which joined the fleet after the start of hostilities

THE IMPERIAL JAPANESE NAVY, FEBRUARY 5, 1904

First Fleet (Vice Admiral Togo Heihachiro)

First Squadron

Battleships *Mikasa, Asahi, Fuji, Yashima, Shikishima, Hatsuse*

Unprotected cruiser *Tatsuta*

Third Squadron

Second-class (protected) cruisers *Chitose, Kasagi, Takasago, Yoshino*

1st Destroyer Division: Destroyers *Shirakumo, Asashio, Kasumi, Akatsuki*

2nd Destroyer Division: Destroyers *Ikazuchi, Oboro, Inadzuma, Akebono*

3rd Destroyer Division: Destroyers *Usugumo, Shinonome, Sazanami*

1st Torpedo Boat Division: Torpedo Boats *67, 68, 69, 70*

14th Torpedo Boat Division: Torpedo Boats *Chidori, Hayabusa, Manadzuru, Kasasagi*

Second Fleet (Vice Admiral Kamimura Hikonojo)

Second Squadron

First-class (armored) cruisers *Idzumo, Adzuma, Asama, Yakumo, Tokiwa, Iwate*

Unprotected cruiser *Chihaya*

Fourth Squadron

Second-class cruisers *Naniwa, Takachiho, Niitaka, Akashi*

4th Destroyer Division: Destroyers *Hayatori, Harusame, Murasame, Asagiri*

5th Destroyer Division: Destroyers *Kagero, Murakumo, Yugiri, Shiranui*

9th Torpedo Boat Division: Torpedo Boats *Aotaka, Hato, Kari, Tsubame*

20th Torpedo Boat Division: Torpedo Boats *62, 63, 64, 65*

Third Fleet (Vice Admiral Kataoka Shichiro)

Fifth Squadron

Second-class battleship *Chin Yen*; second-class cruisers *Itsukushima, Hashidate, Matsushima*

Sixth Squadron

Third-class cruisers *Idzumi, Suma, Akitsushima, Chiyoda*

Seventh Squadron

Third-class battleship *Fuso*; coastal defense ships *Kaimon, Saiyen*; gunboats *Heiyen, Tsukushi, Banjo, Chokai, Atago, Maya, Uji*; unprotected cruiser *Miyako*

10th Torpedo Boat Division: Torpedo Boats *40, 41, 42, 43*

11th Torpedo Boat Division: Torpedo Boats *72, 73, 74, 75*

16th Torpedo Boat Division: Torpedo Boats *Shirataka, 39, 66, 71*

Guard and Patrol Forces

Unprotected Cruiser *Yaeyama*

Coastal Defense Ships *Takao, Tenryu, Katsuragi, Yamato, Musashi*

1st Torpedo Boat Division: Torpedo Boats *44, 47, 48, 49*

2nd Torpedo Boat Division: Torpedo Boats *37, 38, 45, 46*

3rd Torpedo Boat Division: Torpedo Boats *15, 20, 54, 55*

4th Torpedo Boat Division: Torpedo Boats *5, 6, 7, 8, 9*

5th Torpedo Boat Division: Torpedo Boats *Fukuryu, 25, 26, 27*

6th Torpedo Boat Division: Torpedo Boats *56, 57, 58, 59*

7th Torpedo Boat Division: Torpedo Boats *11, 12, 13, 14*

8th Torpedo Boat Division: Torpedo Boats *10, 17, 18, 19*

12th Torpedo Boat Division: Torpedo Boats *50, 51, 52, 53*

13th Torpedo Boat Division: Torpedo Boats *Kotaka, 21, 24, 29, 30*

15th Torpedo Boat Division (formed on February 10 and later assigned to 3rd Fleet):

Torpedo Boats *Hibari, Sagi, Uzura, Hashitaka*

17th Torpedo Boat Division: Torpedo Boats *31, 32, 33, 34*

18th Torpedo Boat Division: Torpedo Boats *35, 36, 60, 61*

19th Torpedo Boat Division (formed in May 1904 and later assigned to 2nd Fleet):

Torpedo Boats *Otori, Kamome, Kiji*

The destroyer *Kasumi* in 1902. This ship was celebrated in the IJN as she was credited with torpedoing a Russian cruiser in the opening attack at Port Arthur. As an improved Ikazuchi-class ship, she retained the same basic configuration as that class. Most early classes had their gun battery modified with the addition of a second 3in gun fitted on the small forward superstructure in place of the centerline 57mm mount. (*Ships of the World* Magazine)

The Russian Pacific Fleet was divided into two parts. The bulk of the fleet was located in Port Arthur. This was an ice-free port near the west coast of Korea where the Japanese landings would take place. However, Port Arthur lacked robust repair facilities. The other major Russian Far East port, Vladivostok, although possessing more developed repair facilities, was iced-in for part of the year and was remote from the focus of the action on the west coast of Korea. The IJN decided to screen the small Russian force based there with light forces.

THE IJN IN THE RUSSO-JAPANESE WAR

The Attack at Port Arthur

To open the war, the IJN decided on a direct attack on Port Arthur. After some debate between Togo and the Naval General Staff, it was decided to attack the Russian fleet anchored in the roadstead with the entire Combined Fleet. The attack would be led by destroyers conducting a surprise night attack with torpedoes. These ships had been practicing the tactics of such an attack since 1902. The entire operation would proceed without a declaration of war.

The destroyers approached Port Arthur on the night of February 8/9 and, just after midnight, they raced toward the Russian fleet which was at anchor. The Japanese achieved total surprise and some Russian ships were fully illuminated. Nevertheless, the results were disappointing. Of the 16 torpedoes launched, only three hit a target; the battleships *Retvizan* and *Tsesarevich* were hit and damaged, along with protected cruiser *Pallada*. The attack was marred by a lack of coordination among the destroyers and a faulty torpedo doctrine which relied on fire from long range.

Togo was not eager to follow up the torpedo attack with his battle fleet. His battleships did not make an appearance off Port Arthur until about noon on February 9, by which time the Russians had recovered from their surprise and were able to sortie their remaining five battleships. More importantly, the shore batteries that Togo feared opened fire in support and, after an indecisive gunnery duel, Togo withdrew without inflicting any real damage

THE ATTACK ON PORT ARTHUR

The IJN planned to open the war against the Russian Pacific Squadron with a crippling surprise attack. The 1st, 2nd and 3rd Destroyer Divisions were ordered to attack the Russian ships anchored in the outer roadstead at Port Arthur on the night of February 8/9, 1904. Ten destroyers headed to the attack, but on their approach they were scattered which meant a massed attack was not possible. The 1st Division (*Shirakumo, Asashio, Kasumi, Akatsuki* with *Ikazuchi* from the 2nd Division) came in first and got to within about 650 yards of the Russian ships and fired nine torpedoes. One of these, from *Kasumi*, hit the cruiser *Pallada*. This scene depicts *Kasumi* firing at the Russian cruiser which is lit and is using her searchlights to illuminate the roadstead. The first attack was followed by two more waves of destroyers, with the five ships firing a total of seven torpedoes. In addition to the hit on *Pallada*, the battleships *Retvizan* and *Tsesarevich* were each hit by a torpedo and seriously damaged. However, the results could have been better. Two destroyer divisions were sent to attack Dalnyy but found no Russian ships present.

Hatsuse in January 1901, the month she was commissioned into service. The ship had a short service life, being mined in May 1904, the second IJN battleship to be lost in this manner. (*Ships of the World* Magazine)

on the Russian fleet. Four of the Japanese battleships and three cruisers were hit during the action. The failure of the opening Japanese attack left the Russian Port Arthur squadron as a serious threat; for the next ten months, the IJN's operations were focused on neutralizing it.

The Siege of Port Arthur

From his fleet anchorage on the western coast of Korea, Togo was forced to conduct a distant blockade of Port Arthur to protect the movement of troops and supplies to Korea. During this period, Togo employed several methods to attack the Russian fleet including torpedo attack by destroyers on many occasions. The attacks were launched at long range, and resulted in no damage until December 1904 when the last Russian battleship anchored outside the harbor was subjected to intensive torpedo attack. Another method employed by the IJN was long-range gunnery attacks by battleships which on three occasions were moved to the other side of the Liaodung Peninsula across from Port Arthur and which fired their 12in guns at the harbor over 15,000 yards away. With no reliable method of observing their fire, this tactic was largely unsuccessful and soon countered by the Russians firing their battleship guns from Port Arthur.

A bolder step was the use of block-ships to seal the narrow entrance to the port. This was considered for the opening attack, but now had to wait until February 23, 1905. The first attempt with five ships failed. Another attempt on March 26 with four ships came closer to success, but also ended in failure. On May 3, an all-out attempt was made with 12 block-ships but this attempt was a complete failure and took a heavy toll on the volunteer crews.

Much more effective was the use of mines. On the night of April 12/13, the Japanese laid a minefield in the waters right off Port Arthur and the results were immediate; the following morning a Russian force ran into the minefield. The Russian flagship, the battleship *Petropavlovsk*, struck a mine and sank immediately. Among those lost was the new commander of the Russian Pacific Fleet, Admiral Stepan Makarov, who was considered the most dynamic of Russian naval leaders. His death was pivotal since it condemned the Russian fleet in Port Arthur to a defensive stance.

In return, the Combined Fleet suffered severe blows from Russian mines. On May 15, two of the six Japanese battleships, *Hatsuse* and *Yashima*, were sunk in a single day. This was a devastating blow since these ships were irreplaceable, and their loss placed the IJN into a position of permanent battleship inferiority against the Russians and

Asahi pictured on August 10, 1904, the day of the battle of the Yellow Sea. The ship presents a worn appearance which was the result of having to remain at sea or at anchorage to enforce the blockade of Port Arthur. Note the heavy secondary battery of seven port-side 6in guns. (*Ships of the World* Magazine)

made Togo even more reluctant to risk his battle fleet. Russian mines were the single most effective weapon used against the IJN during the war.

In the long run, the most severe threat to the Russian fleet in Port Arthur was from an overland attack. By June, the Imperial Army had advanced to within a few miles of Port Arthur but was stopped by Russian machine guns on the heights surrounding the port. The possibility that the Japanese would seize one of the hills overlooking the port and then bring down observed fire on the Russian fleet made the Russian position untenable. The solution, ordered by the Tsar, was to move the Pacific Fleet from Port Arthur to Vladivostok.

The Battle of the Yellow Sea

Following the failure of a half-hearted attempt on June 23, 1905 to reach Vladivostok, the new commander of the Russian 1st Pacific Squadron (renamed as such on April 17, 1904, when elements of the Baltic Fleet were designated the 2nd Pacific Squadron), Rear Admiral Vilgelm Vitgeft, sortied from Port Arthur on August 10. For this operation the Russians mustered a force of six battleships, four cruisers and eight destroyers. The Japanese enjoyed a numerical advantage in all but battleships, but were caught with their forces dispersed. Togo assembled a force of four battleships and placed the armored cruisers *Nisshin* and *Kasuga* in the battle line. Just after noon, the fleets spotted each other and an hour later the Japanese opened fire at long range. After a series of maneuvers, the Russians appeared to gain an advantage and Togo was forced into a stern chase to prevent the Russians from getting away in the few remaining hours of daylight. After a two-hour delay in the action, Togo closed to within range for his force to engage the rearmost Russian battleship. Both sides landed blows with their 12in main batteries and *Mikasa* came in for particular attention which brought her to the verge of being forced to leave the battle.

The battle seemed lost for the Japanese when, at 1840hrs, a salvo from battleship *Asahi* landed on the bridge of the Russian flagship, *Tsesarevich*. The two 12in shells killed Vitgeft and jammed the helm which threw the entire Russian force into confusion. Vitgeft's replacement eventually ordered a return to Port Arthur. With the Russians no longer heading to Vladivostok, Togo played it safe and broke his battleships off which brought an end to the main action. Five Russian battleships returned to Port Arthur, and one was interned at the British port of Kiaochou. Two of the four cruisers were also interned in neutral ports; one returned to Port Arthur, and the final ship made it to Vladivostok. The ships returning to Port Arthur were doomed. Following the capture of a key hill overlooking the harbor on December 5, all but battleship *Sevastopol* were sunk by gunfire. On January 2, 1905,

The Japanese battle line in action on August 10, 1904 at the battle of the Yellow Sea. This view includes all four Japanese battleships with *Shikishima* nearest the camera. Having already lost two battleships, Togo was forced to fight a conservative battle which was only won by a lucky hit on the Russian flagship late in the battle. (Yamato Museum)

Mikasa pictured in February 1905 in readiness for the climactic battle against the Second Russian Pacific Squadron. Note the starboard-side battery of seven 6in guns; these quick-firing weapons proved devastating against the Russian ships. (Yamato Museum)

Sevastopol was scuttled to avoid capture by the Japanese. All were raised after the war and entered service in the IJN.

Battles with the Vladivostok Squadron

While Togo's main efforts were directed at the trapped Russian squadron in Port Arthur, he soon had a new concern. The small Russian force in Vladivostok, built around three powerful and fast armored cruisers, was creating havoc in the Japanese maritime lines of communication in the Sea of Japan. The IJN's original plan was to dedicate the Third Fleet to defending these important sea lanes, but this force's slow and aging ships made it ineffective in this role. Between February and August 1904, the boldly handled Vladivostok squadron made seven sorties into the Sea of Japan. The raids in June and July created real concerns for Japanese shipping and the safety of the sea lanes to Korea, forcing the IJN to change its plans.

To counter this growing threat, the IJN was forced to commit a squadron of armored cruisers from the Second Fleet. After several failed attempts to intercept the marauding Russians, primarily due to weather conditions, Admiral Kamimura and his four armored cruisers finally brought the three Russian armored cruisers to battle on August 14 off the southeast coast of Korea. In a three-hour gun duel named the battle of Ulsan, the IJN sank one Russian armored cruiser and badly damaged the other two. Though the damaged ships were able to return to Vladivostok, they never became a threat to Japanese sea lanes again.

Preparations for the Decisive Battle

The fall of Port Arthur meant the destruction of Russian naval power in the Far East, but not the end of the naval war. The Russians had decided to send their Baltic Fleet to the Far East; on October 15 this large but unwieldy force finally left the Baltic and began an epic eight-month voyage. This gave the IJN plenty of time to prepare; all major ships were sent into the yards for overhaul and improvement. By February 1905, the entire Combined Fleet was in a high state of material readiness.

By early April, the fleet was brought up to a state of combat readiness. Operating out of Chinhae Bay on the southeastern coast of Korea, Togo instituted a program of constant drills and exercises. Either as single ships,

B

THE BATTLE OF TSUSHIMA

The battle of Tsushima was the seminal moment in the IJN's history. The decisive defeat of the Russians enshrined the battle as an enduring element in Japanese naval thinking and strategy. The view here shows the beginning of the gunnery duel between the two combatants. By May 1905, only four of the IJN's original six modern battleships remained. Here they are shown engaging the Russians in the opening moments of the battle. The IJN battle line comprised Togo's flagship *Mikasa* leading *Shikishima*, *Fuji*, and *Asahi*. Russian shells splash all around as the Japanese ships return fire to starboard. In the initial phases of the battle, Russian gunnery was fairly good, but the weight of fire from the better-trained Japanese ships proved decisive.

small groups, or as an entire fleet, Togo's units practiced all the elements required to execute the IJN's battle plan against the larger Russian fleet. Gunnery and torpedo combat was emphasized, but so were communications and formation maneuvering. This rigorous program brought the fleet to an excellent state of combat readiness, and made it much more capable than its Russian opponents. Morale in the fleet was also at a high point.

For the Japanese, the stakes were high. Unless the Russian fleet was decisively defeated, the war would drag on. Japan's strength both at sea and on the ground in Manchuria was waning, and a prolonged conflict meant a peace settlement increasingly less favorable for Japan. In contrast to the war's only previous fleet action at the battle of the Yellow Sea, Togo would have to close with the Russians and destroy them. The Japanese envisioned a two-day battle of annihilation which would begin with destroyer and torpedo boat attacks as the Russians entered the Tsushima Strait, followed by the main attack by the entire fleet in the strait during daylight. In this fleet action, the Japanese battleships were charged to pin down the main Russian force, while the Japanese cruisers attacked and destroyed the rest of the Russian fleet. With darkness, the Japanese would unleash their destroyers and torpedo boats. At dawn of the following day, the main fleet action would begin again and result in the final destruction of the Russian fleet.

The Battle of Tsushima

The Japanese feared that the Russian fleet would seize a base somewhere on the Chinese coast and begin to operate in the East China Sea and Yellow Sea. This would prolong the war and force the IJN to come south to seek action. The Japanese were also unsure about which approach the Russians would take to get to Vladivostok, but planned on the Russians coming through the Tsushima Strait. In the end, the Russians acted as the Japanese expected giving Togo the chance to execute his well-planned set-piece battle.

On the morning of 27 May, an IJN auxiliary cruiser spotted the Russian fleet in the western approaches to the Tsushima Strait. The weather did not permit torpedo boat attacks, so it was up to Togo's main fleet to stop the Russians. At about 0630hrs, the Combined Fleet departed Chinhae and headed southeast. Just after 1400hrs, the two fleets were in close proximity to each other and Togo boldly ordered a turn, keeping his flagship in the lead of the Japanese formation and bringing his entire fleet parallel with the Russian fleet. The Russians opened fire at 1408hrs, as the Japanese executed their turn, but failed to score. The Japanese held their fire until the range had decreased to about 7,000 yards, and then opened fire at 1411hrs. Both sides rained fire on the other, with both scoring hits, but by 1440hrs the Russian fleet turned away to gain some relief. The Japanese gunfire was devastating; one Russian battleship capsized at 1510hrs and the Russian flagship was crippled and later sank. The initial gunnery duel gave the Japanese the upper hand, but Russian gunnery was also accurate, hitting flagship *Mikasa* continually.

After a lull forced by confusion and poor visibility, just after 1800hrs the Japanese located the now re-formed Russian fleet and opened fire. Another Russian battleship capsized at 1850hrs, followed by another which suffered a magazine explosion and blew up at 1920hrs. With the arrival of darkness, Japanese destroyers took over and delivered attacks that finished off the Russian flagship and sank two additional battleships. The next morning, the remaining Russian ships were surrounded by Togo's battle fleet and opted to surrender. The scale of the Japanese victory was breathtaking. The Russian fleet had entered the Tsushima Strait with 38 ships; of these, 34 had been sunk, captured or elected to proceed to a neutral port for internment. Personnel casualties were high with some 4,830 dead and 5,917 captured. Japanese losses were exceedingly minor in comparison – 110 dead with three torpedo boats lost, and three battleships and eight destroyers and torpedo boats damaged.

The victory at Tsushima embedded itself into the IJN's psyche. Togo's battle fleet enjoyed greater speed and, combined with intense training, allowed the Japanese to maneuver effortlessly around the ponderous Russians to bring their superior gunnery to bear. The homogeneity of the Japanese battle fleet was also a big factor. The Japanese emphasis on training clearly paid off, allowing a smaller force to overcome a larger one.

Further, although torpedoes themselves were still primitive, with only two percent of torpedoes fired against moving ships finding a target, the Japanese faith in destroyers armed with torpedoes which could threaten the largest battleship only grew.

Most of all, Tsushima confirmed the notion that naval wars could be decided by a decisive battle of annihilation. The instrument of victory would be the big guns aboard battleships. Because Japan would likely fight against stronger opponents, another lesson was that its ships, but especially its battleships, had to be superior. In a battle against a larger opponent, there had to be a period of attrition, though at Tsushima the battle was won without one. These became articles of faith for the IJN. It was also a fatal legacy when applied to the IJN's next opponent, the United States Navy.

SHIPS OF THE IMPERIAL JAPANESE NAVY

Battleships

The IJN's naval program of 1896 was significant since it provided for four battleships which were more powerful than any others afloat because of their improved armament and armor. Even at this point, the Japanese were seeking ways to compensate for their numerical inferiority compared to other naval powers by building ships with a qualitative edge. This was to become a standard IJN approach for its entire history.

The first two battleships, *Fuji* and *Yashima*, were ordered to counterbalance the two Chinese battleships, so they were already under construction before the formulation of the 1896 expansion plan. The first two ships were based on the Royal Navy's Royal Sovereign class but were faster, and were fitted with more powerful guns which also had a greater rate of fire. The four newer ships were based on the British Majestic class, but were incrementally improved. All six of the IJN's battleships were compatible in terms of speed and firepower which made for a homogeneous battle line. Rounding out the IJN's force of battleships were two old ships which were only suitable for coastal defense.

Fuji and *Yashima*

The IJN's first two battleships were built in Great Britain and did not arrive in time for the Sino-Japanese War. They did provide the backbone of the fleet for the war against Russia. Though these ships were improved from the

Fuji pictured early in her career. Note the main battery of 12in guns in two twin turrets. The secondary port-side battery of five 6in guns is also visible, and four of the 47mm guns are visible in the fighting tops of the two masts. (*Ships of the World* Magazine)

British Royal Sovereign class by the addition of extra armor protection, as with all pre-dreadnoughts, the ships lacked adequate underwater protection. This was demonstrated when *Yashima* was mined and sunk in 1904.

Ship	Builder	Laid down	Launched	Commissioned
Fuji	Thames Iron Works	Aug 1, 1894	Mar 31, 1896	Aug 17, 1897
Yashima	Armstrong Whitworth	Dec 28, 1894	Feb 28, 1996	Sep 9, 1897

Fuji had a long career. During the war with Russia she participated in the attack on Port Arthur in February 1904 where she was hit twice. On March 22, she and *Yashima* used their 12in guns to conduct a long-range bombardment of Port Arthur. She was present at the battles of the Yellow Sea and Tsushima; at Tsushima she was credited with delivering the final, fatal blows against the Russian battleship *Borodino*.

Yashima was also present at Port Arthur in February 1904, and was then used to conduct long-range bombardment of the port in March. On May 15, as part of a task force with *Hatsuse* and *Shikishima*, she ran into a newly placed Russian minefield and hit two mines. The ship was taken under tow but sank that evening before reaching the nearest anchorage; this disaster was kept secret until spring 1905.

BELOW *Shikishima* shown early in her career. The ship incorporated several improvements in protection and secondary armament and was easily discernible by her three stacks. The battleship was present at every major action of the war. (*Ships of the World* Magazine)

Fuji and *Yashima* Specifications	
Displacement	*Fuji* 12,533 tons normal; *Yashima* 12,320 tons normal
Dimensions	Length 412ft overall; beam: *Fuji* 73ft 3in, *Yashima* 73ft 9in; draft: *Fuji* 26ft 6in, *Yashima* 26ft 3in
Propulsion	*Fuji* ten boilers, *Yashima* 14; producing 10,000 natural and 14,000 forced indicated horse power (IHP)
Speed	18kts
Range	4,000nm at 10kts
Protection	Main belt 18in, thinning to 16 and 14in at the ends; upper belt 4in; bulkheads 14in forward, 12in aft; deck 2.5in; barbettes 14in upper, 9in lower; main turrets and casemates 6in; conning tower 14in
Armament	four 12in/40, ten 6in/40, 20 47mm (in 1901, 16 replaced with 3in), four 47mm, five 18in torpedo tubes (TT) (one on the bow above water, four submerged)
Crew	637 as built rising to 741

Shikishima, Hatsuse, and Asahi

The IJN's next three battleships were also built in Great Britain. The design was an improved British Majestic class, but the modifications made by the Japanese made them clearly superior ships. They were also much improved in firepower with the addition of four 6in guns and a large battery of quick-firing 3in guns. *Shikishima* and *Hatsuse* featured three stacks, making them the only IJN battleships during the war to have this appearance.

Ship	Builder	Laid down	Launched	Commissioned
Shikishima	Thames Iron Works	Mar 29, 1897	Nov 1, 1898	Jan 26, 1900
Hatsuse	Armstrong Whitworth	Jan 10, 1898	Jun 27, 1899	Jan 18, 1901
Asahi	J. Brown	Aug 1, 1898	Mar 13, 1899	Jul 31, 1900

Hatsuse pictured in February/March 1902 in her pre-war paint scheme. Immediately before the start of war, all major IJN ships were painted in a dark-gray scheme which was retained up to the Pacific War and is similar to the current color of Japanese Maritime Self Defense Force ships. (Yamato Museum)

Protection was stressed in these ships. *Shikishima* was sturdily built with a double bottom and a total of 261 watertight compartments. On *Asahi*, this was increased to 55 compartments in the double bottom and 233 watertight compartments above it. The armored scheme was altered with the introduction of Harvey nickel steel, which provided 33 percent more protection than earlier plates of the same thickness. This meant that the main belt could be reduced to 9in while still providing the same degree of protection as the thicker belt on *Fuji*. The weight of armor saved meant the main belt could be further extended on its ends and that the upper belt could be increased to 6in. Another improvement was the design of the armored deck which sloped down on the sides which augmented the vertical protection. The flat middle portion of the armor deck was increased to 4in. *Asahi* had minor alterations to her protection scheme including extensions to the main belt.

Asahi in 1900, the year she was delivered to the IJN. The ship is in a light-gray scheme which was worn by major ships until September 1901. The forward 12in turret is trained to starboard, but much of the secondary armament is behind watertight doors in the hull or main deck casemates. (Yamato Museum)

Hatsuse was a near-sister with modifications to her quick-firing guns and no bow torpedo tube. *Asahi* was similar to *Shikishima* but had only two stacks and there were variations on the placement of her quick-firing small guns.

Shikishima was one of the IJN's stalwart ships during the war. During the opening attack on Port Arthur she was hit by a shell which wounded 17 crew. She was present at the battle of the Yellow Sea where she was again damaged by a single shell. At Tsushima she was hit six times which wounded 13 and killed 24.

Hatsuse was the most important IJN ship lost during the war. During the bombardment of Port Arthur on February 9, 1904 she took two hits which killed 14 and wounded 16. Her short combat career came to a close when on May 15, 1904 she struck a mine under her stern which flooded the steering compartment. *Asahi* took her in tow and it looked like she would be saved. However, *Hatsuse* hit a second mine which detonated a magazine and sent her to the bottom in only minutes with the loss of 493 men.

Asahi was also very active during the war. At the battle of the Yellow Sea she was heavily engaged but emerged undamaged. She had the distinction of being one of the few pre-dreadnoughts to survive damage from a mine; on October 26, 1904, a mine exploded against her belt. Thanks to her sturdy construction, she survived and was repaired in time to rejoin the fleet before Tsushima. At this final battle, she was hit twice and suffered eight dead and 23 wounded.

Shikishima, Hatsuse, and *Asahi* Specifications

Displacement	*Shikishima* 14,850 tons normal, *Hatsuse* 15,000 tons, *Asahi* 15,200 tons; *Shikishima* 15,453 tons full load, *Hatsuse* 15,255 tons, *Asahi* 15,374 tons
Dimensions	Length: *Shikishima* 438ft overall, *Hatsuse* 439ft 9in, *Asahi* 425ft 6in; beam: *Shikishima* 75ft 6in, *Hatsuse* 76ft 9in, *Asahi* 75ft 3in; draft: *Shikishima* and *Asahi* 27ft 3in, *Hatsuse* 27ft
Propulsion	Twenty-five boilers producing 14,500 IHP (*Hatsuse* and *Asahi* 15,000 IHP)
Speed	18kts
Range	4,000nm at 10kts
Protection	Main belt 9in, thinning to 4in at the ends; upper belt 6in with 6in bulkheads; bulkheads 12/14in; deck 4in flat, 2.5in sloped sides; barbettes 14in upper, 10in lower; main turrets and casemates 6in; conning tower 14in
Armament	four 12in/40, 14 6in/40, 20 3in, six 47mm (*Hatsuse* eight 47mm); *Shikishima* five 18in TT (one on the bow above water, four submerged), *Hatsuse* and *Asahi* no bow tube
Crew	*Shikishima* and *Asahi* 836, *Hatsuse* 741

Mikasa

Mikasa was Togo's flagship throughout the Russo-Japanese War. Because the tactics of the day called for the flagship to lead the formation, she came in for concentrated Russian attention during both major battles and received heavy damage at the battles of the Yellow Sea and Tsushima. She led the IJN to victory and has been maintained as a museum ship since 1926, making her one of the IJN's most famous ships.

Since she was the last of the battleships built in Great Britain, she had the most advanced protection scheme. She was the only IJN battleship with Krupp cemented armor plate. Protection for the 6in-gun secondary battery was improved and a splinter deck with one inch of steel was raised to the upper deck to give some protection to the 3in battery.

Mikasa in March 1902 around the time she was delivered to the IJN. As the most modern battleship in the IJN, she assumed the role of the flagship of the Combined Fleet and fought in every major action of the war. (*Ships of the World* Magazine)

Ship	Builder	Laid down	Launched	Commissioned
Mikasa	Armstrong Whitworth	Jan 24, 1899	Nov 8, 1900	Mar 1, 1902

Mikasa stood up well to the pounding she received as Togo's flagship. On February 9, 1904, she received two large-caliber hits while bombarding Port Arthur. At the battle of the Yellow Sea she took an astounding 25 hits which killed 31 and wounded 94. The damage put her 12in battery out of action. At Tsushima, she took an even greater pounding with 32 hits (including ten large-caliber rounds) which killed or wounded 113.

On September 12, 1905, *Mikasa* sank in Sasebo due to a magazine explosion; the cause was determined to be unstable powder. She was raised on August 7, 1906 and placed back into service in 1907. The IJN was extremely fortunate that this accident did not occur during the war.

Mikasa **Specifications**	
Displacement	15,140 tons normal; 15,179 full load
Dimensions	Length 432ft overall; beam 76ft; draft 27ft 2in
Propulsion	Twenty-five boilers producing 15,000 IHP
Speed	18kts
Range	5,300nm at 10kts
Protection	Main belt 9in, thinning to 4in at the ends; upper belt 6in with 6in bulkheads; bulkheads 12/14in; deck 2in flat, 3in sloped sides; barbettes 14in upper, 10in lower; main turrets and casemates 6in; conning tower 14in
Armament	four 12in/40, 14 6in/40, 20 3in, eight 47mm; four 18in TT (all submerged)
Crew	830

Second-class battleship *Chin Yen*

The IJN's first battleship was the ex-Chinese German-built *Chin Yen*. The ship was salvaged from the port of Wei-Hei-Wei after its fall to the Japanese in February 1895. The ship was heavily armored and equipped with four 12in guns. She and a sister ship of identical design gave a good account of themselves during the first Sino-Japanese War. At the battle of the Yalu River she was struck by hundreds of shells from the IJN's quick-firing guns, but none penetrated her main armor. After being captured, the ship was re-armed by the Japanese. During the Russo-Japanese War, she did not see action and was stricken in 1911.

Chin Yen seen here in 1898. She was captured from the Chinese in 1895 and placed into service as the IJN's first battleship. Though heavily protected, the layout of her armament was antiquated, and she saw only second-line service during the war. (*Ships of the World Magazine*)

Ship	Builder	Laid down	Launched	Commissioned
Chin Yen	Vulcan (Stettin)	?	1882	1884

Chin Yen **(1904) Specifications**	
Displacement	7,220 tons normal
Dimensions	Length 308ft overall; beam 59ft; draft 20ft
Propulsion	6,200 IHP
Speed	14.5kts
Range	4,500nm at 10 knots
Protection	Main belt 10–14in, bulkheads 14in; deck 3in; barbettes 12in; conning tower 8in
Armament	four 12in/20, four 6in/40, two 57mm, eight 47mm; three 14in TT
Crew	250

Fuso pictured in April 1900. Delivered as the IJN's first armored ship in 1878, she was clearly outdated by the Russo-Japanese War and saw no action. The ship's primary armament of two 6in guns can be seen in single mounts fore and aft. (Yamato Museum)

Third-class battleship *Fuso*

The first armored ship to be built in Great Britain for the IJN was *Fuso*. The ship arrived in Japan in 1878 and fought in the battle of the Yalu River in 1894 and was still in service when the war against the Russians began. By this time she had been re-armed and redesignated as a coastal defense ship. She was finally taken out of service in 1907.

Fuso (1904) Specifications	
Displacement	3,717 tons normal
Dimensions	Length 220ft overall; beam 48ft; draft 20ft
Propulsion	Eight boilers producing 3,932 IHP
Speed	13kts
Range	4,500nm at 10kts
Protection	Main belt 9in, thinning to 4in at the ends; bulkheads 8in; battery 8in
Armament	two 6in/50, four 4.7in/40, 11 57mm, four 47mm; three 18in TT
Crew	386

The IJN's largest and most graceful ships were its armored cruisers, particularly the ones built in Britain. These combined a fairly high degree of protection with a heavy armament and good speed. Shown here is *Asama* in June 1902. The main 8in battery was carried in two twin turrets, and the heavy secondary armament of 14 6in guns was mounted in five hull and main deck casemates per side, with two more provided with shielded mounts. (Yamato Museum)

Armored Cruisers

A major part of the IJN's strength during the war with Russia was its force of modern armored cruisers. The original six armored cruisers called for in the 1897 revision of the naval expansion plan were all built in foreign yards and completed between 1899 and 1901. These were joined by two Italian-built cruisers purchased just before the war. All of these ships were fast and powerfully armed. The Japanese believed that an armored cruiser fitted with the latest Harvey or Krupp armor would be able to provide adequate protection against all but the heaviest projectiles while the armored cruiser's powerful battery of quick-firing medium guns gave it superior firepower compared to a second-class battleship equipped with only slow-firing short-range 12in guns. This assessment proved correct and the IJN's armored cruisers were employed in the battle line at Yellow Sea and Tsushima and proved successful in this role. This ability of the IJN's armored cruisers to operate as part of the battle line was especially important after two of the IJN's six battleships were lost early in the war.

Aside from their exploits during the two major fleet actions, IJN armored cruisers were active throughout the war. At the battle of Chemulpo (modern day Inchon), *Asama* and the IJN's oldest armored cruiser, *Chiyoda*, took the lead role in destroying a Russian armored cruiser and a gunboat. At the battle of Ulsan, armored cruisers *Idzumo*, *Adzuma*, *Tokiwa* and *Iwate*, supported by two protected cruisers, methodically shot up a squadron of three Russian armored cruisers. Two of the Japanese armored cruisers took extensive damage, but remained in action.

Asama and *Tokiwa*

Orders for the first armored cruisers were placed with the Armstrong firm and built at the Elswick yard in Great Britain.

THE BATTLESHIPS

1: The IJN's first battleship, *Fuji*, is shown in 1900 in a light-gray scheme that she wore until late 1901. The ship's main armament can be seen in the form of the two twin 12in turrets fore and aft. The secondary battery of ten 6in guns was distributed five per side; these can be seen amidships with three mounted on the main deck and two below in hull casemates. The 57mm mounts were distributed around the ship. The four 47mm guns were fitted two each in the foremast and mainmast.

2: *Shikishima* as she appeared in 1902, painted in the scheme of a black hull and black upperworks. The ship's overall appearance is similar to *Fuji's*. Differences include three stacks instead of two. The secondary battery has been increased to 14 6in guns with seven per side. Four are mounted in hull casemates and the other three were on the gun deck on the main deck level.

3: *Asahi* is shown in 1905 in a dark-gray wartime scheme. Her appearance was similar to *Shikishima*. The battleship possessed the same main and secondary battery, but has reverted to a two-stack appearance.

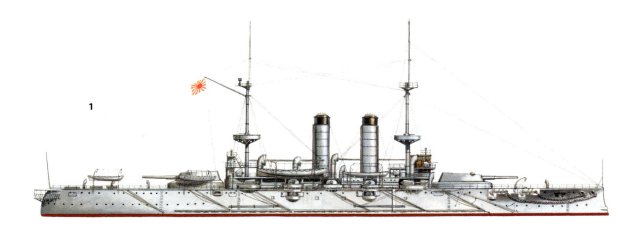

1

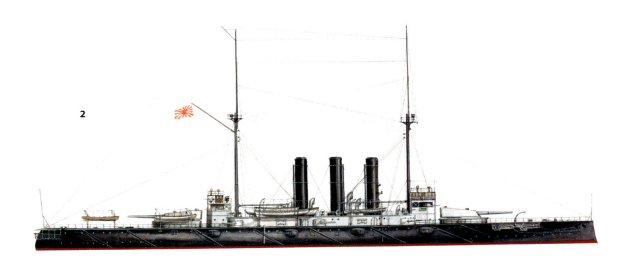

2

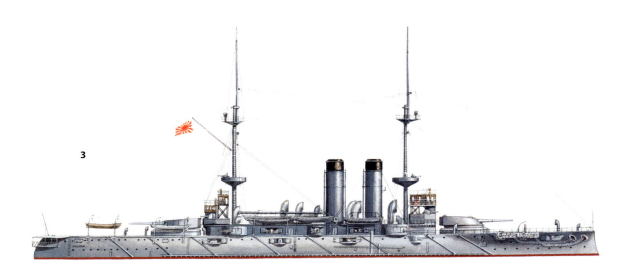

3

Ship	Builder	Laid down	Launched	Commissioned
Asama	Armstrong Elswick	Nov 1896	Mar 22, 1898	Mar 18, 1899
Tokiwa	Armstrong Elswick	Jan 1898	Jul 6, 1898	May 18, 1899

Tokiwa pictured in February 1905 before Tsushima. Both Asama-class armored cruisers were damaged during the battle but continued in action. (*Ships of the World* Magazine)

Both of these ships had good war records. *Asama* opened the war with an action against Russian armored cruiser *Varyag* in Chemulpo in which the Russian ship was extensively damaged and forced to scuttle. *Asama* took part in the unsuccessful attempt in March 1904 to attack the Russian squadron in Vladivostok and was also present at Yellow Sea, joining late in the day. At Tsushima, she was hit 12 times and suffered three dead and 13 wounded.

Tokiwa's war exploits were similar. She took part in the unsuccessful attempts to engage the Port Arthur squadron in February and the Vladivostok squadron in March. In the battle of Ulsan she was heavily engaged but suffered only three hits in return. At Tsushima she was also fortunate and suffered only three hits and 15 casualties.

Asama and *Tokiwa* Specifications	
Displacement	9,700 tons normal; *Asama* 10,519 tons full load; *Tokiwa* 10,476 tons full load
Dimensions	Length 442ft overall; beam 67ft 3in; draft 24ft 6in
Propulsion	Twelve boilers producing 18,000 IHP
Speed	21.5kts
Range	4,600nm at 11.6kts
Protection	Main belt 7in, thinning to 3.5in at the ends and closed by 5in bulkheads; upper belt 5in; deck 2in; barbettes 6in; main turrets and casemates 6in; conning tower 14in
Armament	four 8in/40, 14 6in/40, 12 76mm, seven 57mm; five 18in TT (one in bow above water, four submerged)
Crew	726

Yakumo

The IJN's third armored cruiser was ordered from the Vulcan firm's yard at Stettin in eastern Germany. The ship was the first IJN ship with Krupp armor and benefited from the typical German design attention on sturdiness and compartmentation. To avoid any problems with different ammunition supplies, the ship was fitted with British-built guns from Elswick.

Yakumo in June 1900 before leaving Germany for her trip to Japan. The German-built ship was largely to the same specifications as those built in Britain and, to lessen logistical issues, the IJN specified that the ship should be completed with British-supplied weapons. (*Ships of the World* Magazine)

Ship	Builder	Laid down	Launched	Commissioned
Yakumo	Vulcan	Mar 1898	Jul 8, 1899	Jun 20, 1900

The ship's war record was outstanding. She was credited with hitting a Russian cruiser during the opening attack on Port Arthur. In March 1904, the cruiser bombarded Vladivostok and maintained the blockade of the port the following month. *Yakumo* was present at Yellow Sea where she was hit by a 12in shell and at Tsushima, she and *Iwate* were credited with delivering the final blows that accounted for a Russian battleship; in exchange, she recorded five hits from Russian shells.

Yakumo Specifications	
Displacement:	9,646 tons normal; 10,288 tons full load
Dimensions:	Length 434ft overall; beam 64ft 3in; draft 23ft 9in
Propulsion:	Twenty-four boilers producing 15,500 IHP
Speed:	20.5kts
Range:	4,000nm at 10.7 knots
Protection:	Main belt 7in, thinning to 3.5in at the ends and closed by 5in forward bulkhead; upper belt 5in; deck 2.5in; barbettes 6in; main turrets and casemates 6in; conning tower 14in
Armament:	four 8in/40, 12 6in/40, 12 76mm, seven 57mm; five 18in TT (one in bow above water, four submerged)
Crew:	700

Adzuma

One of the IJN's early suppliers of warships was France; in fact, for a period France was the preferred supplier. This armored cruiser was built in St Nazaire and was similar in performance to the British-built ships, but was slightly inferior in her protection scheme and speed. She could be distinguished by her different-shaped stacks.

The largest ship built for the IJN by French yards was *Adzuma*, pictured here in 1901 after arriving in Japan. The unique shape of her stacks made her readily identifiable. (Yamato Museum)

Ship	Builder	Laid down	Launched	Commissioned
Adzuma	Ateliers et Chentiers de la Loire	Mar 1898	Jun 24, 1899	Jul 28, 1900

Adzuma was present at the initial attack on Port Arthur, and then was assigned to blockade and engage the Russian Vladivostok squadron. She was part of the March bombardment of Vladivostok and at Ulsan was hit ten times. The cruiser demonstrated her toughness at Tsushima by taking another 11 hits with 11 dead and 29 wounded.

Adzuma Specifications	
Displacement	9,307 tons normal; 9,943 tons full load
Dimensions	Length 452ft 6in overall; beam 68ft 9in; draft 23ft 9in
Propulsion	Twenty-four boilers producing 17,000 IHP
Speed	20kts
Range	3,900nm at 10.7kts
Protection	Main belt 7in, thinning to 3.5in at the ends and closed by 3in forward bulkhead; upper belt 5in; deck 2.5in; barbettes 6in; main turrets and casemates 6in; conning tower 14in
Armament	four 8in/40, 12 6in/40, 12 76mm, 12 57mm; five 18in TT (one in bow above water, four submerged)
Crew	650

Idzumo and Iwate

The two ships of this class were built in the same yard as the Asama class but, since they were laid down some 18 months later, they benefited from several minor improvements. Protection was improved with the use of Krupp cemented armor, the armored deck was slightly augmented and the bow torpedo tube was deleted. Compartmentation was extensive with 30 compartments in the double bottom and 136 above. The fitting of 24 boilers necessitated the addition of a third stack which gave these ships a unique

Mikasa as she appeared in May 1905 at the battle of Tsushima. *Mikasa* was the flagship of Admiral Togo throughout the war and was therefore the most famous ship of the pre-World War II IJN. She is preserved today as a museum ship.

appearance among IJN armored cruisers. The machinery plant was improved so that 300 tons of weight was saved but power was unaffected.

Ship	Builder	Laid down	Launched	Commissioned
Idzumo	Armstrong Elswick	May 1898	Sep 19, 1899	Sep 25, 1900
Iwate	Armstrong Elswick	Nov 1898	Mar 29, 1900	Mar 18, 1901

These rugged ships were active during the war and performed well. Both took part in the first bombardment of Port Arthur and both were central at the battle of Ulsan in which Russian armored cruiser *Rurik* was sunk; *Idzumo* recorded 20 hits and *Iwate* was hit 23 times including one hit by an 8in shell which set off ammunition in the casemates, knocking out three 6in guns, killing 40 and wounding 37. *Idzumo* was Kamimura's flagship at Tsushima and took 9 hits; *Iwate* was at the end of the squadron line and took 8 hits.

Idzumo and *Iwate* Specifications	
Displacement	9,750 tons normal; 10,305 tons full load
Dimensions	Length 434ft overall; beam 68ft 9in; draft 24ft 3in
Propulsion	Twenty-four boilers producing 14,500 IHP
Speed	20.75kts
Range	*Idzumo* 4,600nm; *Iwate* 4,500nm at 10kts
Protection	Main belt 7in, thinning to 3.5in at the ends and closed by 5in bulkheads; upper belt 5in; deck 2.5in; barbettes 6in; main turrets and casemates 6in; conning tower 14in
Armament	four 8in/40, 14 6in/40, 12 76mm, eight 57mm; four 18in TT (all submerged)
Crew	672

Kasuga and Nisshin

As war with Russia looked all but certain, the Japanese looked around for other warships they could acquire to provide a quick boost. An attractive possibility was two armored cruisers being built in Italy for Argentina. Since the Argentinians no longer needed them to fight Chile, they came up for sale in late 1903. They were quickly grabbed by the Japanese with the sale finalized on December 29. They were a fine addition to the IJN since they possessed characteristics similar to its other armored cruisers and the guns were British-built which avoided any logistical difficulties. Protection was only slightly less than the IJN's other armored cruisers and used Italian armor plate produced by the Krupp process. *Kasuga* carried a single 10in gun in her forward turret instead of the normal twin 8in gun and both ships carried the more powerful 8in/45 gun which could fire five rounds per minute.

Ship	Builder	Laid down	Launched	Commissioned
Kasuga	Ansaldo	Mar 1902	Oct 1902	Jan 7, 1904
Nisshin	Ansaldo	May 1902	Feb 1903	Jan 7, 1904

These ships had a slightly lower speed than the rest of the IJN's armored cruisers; this, combined with their somewhat heavier armament, made them a natural selection to replace the two mined battleships in Togo's battle line. They did not arrive in Japan until mid-February and did not join the fleet until April 11, 1904. Their first action was a bombardment of Port Arthur on April 14. A month later, *Kasuga* was damaged when she rammed and sank protected cruiser *Yoshino* off Port Arthur. At the battle of the Yellow Sea, *Nisshin* was last in the line of the First Squadron, so came under heavy fire and took three hits which killed 16 and wounded 30. At Tsushima, *Kasuga* engaged a Russian battleship which surrendered while *Nisshin* was again at the rear of the battle line and took nine hits losing three guns, with six dead and 89 wounded.

LEFT *Kasuga* was a useful addition to the IJN's battle line when she was purchased in December 1903. The ship had an unorthodox appearance with widely spaced stacks and a single mast amidships. The forward turret mounted a single 10in gun, also unique among IJN armored cruisers. (*Ships of the World* Magazine)

ABOVE *Nisshin* in June 1905 after the battle of Tsushima. Any sign of damage from the nine hits she incurred during the battle has been repaired. *Nisshin* and *Kasuga* successfully augmented the IJN's battle line at both the Yellow Sea and Tsushima clashes. (Yamato Museum)

Kasuga and Nisshin Specifications	
Displacement	*Kasuga* 7,628 tons normal, 8,591 tons full load; *Nisshin* 7,698 tons normal, 8,384 full load
Dimensions	Length 366ft 6in overall; beam 61ft 6in; draft 24ft
Propulsion	Eight boilers producing 13,500 IHP
Speed	20kts
Range	5,500nm at 10kts
Protection	Main belt 6in, thinning to 2.75in at the ends and closed by 4.75in bulkheads; upper belt 6in; deck 1.5in; barbettes 6in; main turrets and casemates 6in; conning tower 6in
Armament	one 10in/45 (*Kasuga* only), four 8in/45 (*Kasuga* 2), 14 6in/45, ten 76mm, six 57mm; four 18in TT (above waterline)
Crew	600

The Protected Cruisers

Protected cruisers were the most common type of cruiser in the IJN and other navies during the period of the Sino-Japanese War and leading up to the Russo-Japanese War. These ships were fast enough and had the range to perform scouting duties for the main fleet and to be detached for commerce raiding or for commerce protection. To ensure they had the speed to perform these duties, they were left largely unarmored. The IJN followed the lead of the Royal Navy which preferred protected cruisers with an armored deck and

ABOVE *Naniwa* in March 1886 after being commissioned into the IJN. These were the first protected cruisers ordered from British yards and the IJN's first truly modern ships. The original single 10.3in guns fore and aft can be seen here, but by the Russo-Japanese War these slow-firing weapons had been replaced by 6in guns. The old cruiser performed well during the war against the Russians. (Yamato Museum)

RIGHT *Takachiho* in February 1905 just before she fought at Tsushima. The original 10.3in guns are gone, and the ship carried eight 6in guns in single turrets fore and aft and three on each beam. (Yamato Museum)

no belt armor. The thinking behind this was that the belt armor would not be effective in defeating modern armor-piercing guns without being so thick that speed would be impaired. The only real armor was placed on an armored deck which was below the waterline and acted as a splinter deck to protect the vitals of the ship, such as magazines and machinery. Typically, this armored deck was sloped on the ends and flat in the middle. Side protection was provided by the placement of the coal bunkers. The only other protection fitted was in the form of armored shields on the larger guns and to the conning tower. In IJN parlance, protected cruisers were usually classed as second-class cruisers.

Protected cruisers pioneered the use of quick-firing guns. These guns possessed a significant advantage over older weapons since they made use of a cartridge case made of brass instead of cloth which meant that the guns could be reloaded immediately without having to be sponged out. This increased the rate of fire by as much as six times. By the Russo-Japanese War, quick-firing guns were the norm for both sides.

Naniwa and *Takachiho*

The IJN's first protected cruisers were two ships ordered from Great Britain in 1883. Originally the ships were heavily armed with two 10.3in single mounts and six 5.9in guns but, by 1904, these had been replaced with a uniform armament of 6in guns.

 E

THE ARMORED CRUISERS

1: The top profile is the British-built *Asama* as built in 1899. The ship is wearing a light-gray overall scheme. Armored cruisers were large ships, much longer than the battleships of the day. This hull form helped them to attain high speeds. The typical armored cruiser had a main battery of two twin 8in turrets fore and aft and a secondary battery mounted broadside. *Asama* has the two 8in turrets and a powerful battery of 14 6in guns. Seven of these can be seen in the profile; five are in casemates and two in shielded mounts on the main deck.

2: The middle view shows the French-built *Adzuma* in 1900. The ship has the typical armored cruiser configuration, but is readily identifiable by its French-style stacks. In addition to the two twin 8in turrets, the secondary battery of 12 6in/40 guns can be seen. Four of the starboard-side guns are in shielded mounts on the main deck, and only two are in hull casemates.

3: The IJN's final armored cruisers were two Italian-built ships. *Kasuga* is shown in 1905. Without a doubt, these were the IJN's least attractive armored cruisers. They present an overall stubby appearance being some 40ft shorter than the IJN's other armored cruisers, and present a profile dominated by two widely spaced stacks. Unusually, the ship has only a single mast fitted amidships. The main battery was also unusual in that a single 10in gun was mounted forward and the typical twin 8in mounted aft. The secondary 6in/40 battery of 14 guns, seven per side, can be seen with five guns in hull casemates and two in shielded mounts on the main deck.

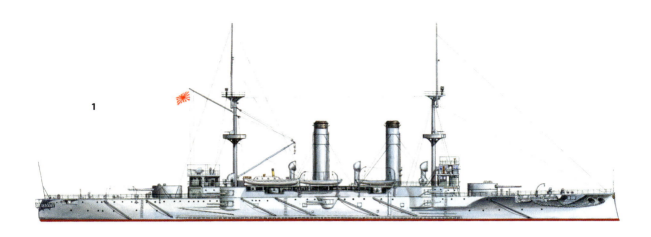

1

2

3

Ship	Builder	Laid down	Launched	Commissioned
Naniwa	Armstrong	Mar 27, 1884	Mar 18, 1885	Jan 1886
Takachiho	Armstrong	Apr 4, 1884	May 16, 1885	Mar 26, 1886

These ships were veterans of the Sino-Japanese War in which they proved successful in action. *Naniwa* fought with her sister ship at the battles of Chemulpo and Ulsan. Both were also present at Tsushima where *Naniwa* was damaged.

Naniwa and *Takachiho* Specifications	
Displacement	3,650 tons normal; 4,150 tons full load
Dimensions	Length 300ft overall; beam 46ft; draft 18ft 6in
Propulsion	Six boilers producing 7,000 IHP
Speed	18.5kts
Range	9,000nm at 13kts
Protection	Armored deck; 3in on sloped sides, 2in central flat portion; gun shields 1.5in; conning tower 1.5in
Armament	eight 6in, two 57mm, ten 37mm, four 14in TT (above waterline)
Crew	325

Itsukushima, Matsushima, and *Hashidate*

This three-ship class included the largest ship built in Japan up to that time, *Hashidate*; the other two ships were built in France. This class proved disappointing in service. The design was centered around a single 12.6in gun which the Japanese felt they needed to deal with the heavy armor of China's two German-built battleships. In exchange for mounting a large gun, protection, speed and seakeeping were sacrificed. The ships fought in the Sino-Japanese War where their slow-firing 12.6in gun proved ineffective.

Ship	Builder	Laid down	Launched	Commissioned
Itsukushima	La Seyne	Jan 1888	Jul 11, 1889	Aug 1891
Matsushima	La Seyne	Feb 1888	Jan 22, 1890	Mar 1891
Hashidate	Yokosuka NY (Navy Yard)	Sep 1888	Mar 24, 1891	Jun 1894

By the Russo-Japanese War, *Matsushima* had her 12.6in gun moved aft in an attempt to improve seakeeping. In spite of their limited capabilities, all three ships were used on blockade duties off Port Arthur and were present at the battles of the Yellow Sea and Tsushima.

BELOW Another veteran of the Sino-Japanese War to see service in the war against the Russians was *Matsushima*. This ship was built around a single 12.6in gun which in service proved unsuccessful. Pictured in 1905, *Matsushima* has had her 12.6in gun moved aft in an attempt to improve seakeeping. (Yamato Museum)

BELOW RIGHT *Hashidate*, shown here in 1907, was the largest ship built in Japan when she was completed in 1894. The ship is dominated by a single 12.6in gun fitted forward. The slow-firing weapon was unsuccessful in service, but the cruiser served well in the war against the Russians. (*Ships of the World* Magazine)

Itsukushima, Matsushima, and Hashidate Specifications

Displacement	4,217 tons normal
Dimensions	Length 301ft overall; beam 51ft 3in; draft 20ft
Propulsion	Six boilers producing 5,400 IHP
Speed	16.5kts
Range	6,000nm at 10kts
Protection	Armored deck 2in; main gun barbette and hoist 12in; main gun shield 4in
Armament	one 12.6in, 11 4.7in/40 (*Matsushima* 12); 5 57mm (*Matsushima* 16); 11 47mm (*Matsushima* none); six 37mm; four 14in TT
Crew	360

Chiyoda

Chiyoda was originally an armored cruiser, but by the Russo-Japanese War was considered by the IJN to be a second-class cruiser, so she is included in this section. The ship was built in Great Britain and was one of the first to carry an armament of all quick-firing guns.

Ship	Builder	Laid down	Launched	Commissioned
Chiyoda	Thomson	Nov 1888	Jun 1890	Dec 1890

Chiyoda, seen here in 1892, was the IJN's first armored cruiser. By 1904, she was showing her age with a weak main battery of 4.7in guns and protection in no way comparable to modern armored cruisers. In spite of her age and limited capabilities, she was active during the war, and even survived hitting a mine. (Yamato Museum)

Chiyoda was another veteran of the battle of the Yalu River in 1894. In 1904, she was present off Chemulpo when the war began and engaged a Russian gunboat. On July 27, she struck a mine, but was salvaged. She returned to service in time to participate in the battle of Tsushima.

Chiyoda Specifications

Displacement	2,400 tons normal
Dimensions	Length 310ft overall; beam 42ft 6in; draft 14ft
Propulsion	Six boilers producing 5,600 IHP
Speed	19kts
Range	8,000nm at 10kts
Protection	Main belt 4.5in; armored deck 1in
Armament	ten 4.7in/40, 14 47mm, three 14in TT above waterline
Crew	350

Akitsushima

Ship	Builder	Laid down	Launched	Commissioned
Akitsushima	Yokosuka NY.	Mar 1890	Jul 1892	Feb 1894

Akitsushima pictured in 1897 was based on an American design, but had mediocre armament and speed. She fought against both the Chinese and the Russians. (*Ships of the World* Magazine)

Akitsushima was built to a design similar to that of the USN protected cruiser *Baltimore*. The ship was built in Japan with imported steel, making her the last major warship constructed in this manner. The ship proved less than satisfactory in service. She was present at the battle of the Yalu River and then at Tsushima where she was damaged by a single shell hit.

Akitsushima Specifications

Displacement	3,100 tons normal
Dimensions	Length 301ft overall; beam 43ft; draft 17ft 6in
Propulsion	Four boilers producing 8,400 IHP
Speed	19kts
Range	Unknown
Protection	Armored deck 3in; gun shields 4.5in
Armament	four 6in/40, six 4.7in/40, eight 47mm, four 14in TT above watrerline
Crew	330

Yoshino

Ship	Builder	Laid down	Launched	Commissioned
Yoshino	Armstrong	Feb 1892	Dec 20, 1892	Sep 1893

Yoshino was another British design and was a symbol of the growing IJN when she entered service. She was among the fastest cruisers of her day when commissioned and carried an armament of all quick-firing guns. She was present at the battle of the Yalu River; during the Russo-Japanese War she was sunk early in the conflict when she was rammed by armored cruiser *Kasuga* on May 15, 1904 near Port Arthur with the loss of most of her crew.

Yoshino Specifications

Displacement	4,150 tons normal
Dimensions	Length 360ft; beam 46ft 6in; draft 17ft
Propulsion	Twelve boilers producing 15,000 IHP
Speed	23kts
Range	9,000nm at 10kts
Protection	Armored deck 4.5in on the ends, 1.75in on flat section; gun shields 4.5in
Armament	four 6in/40, eight 4.7in/40, 22 47mm, five 14in TT above waterline
Crew	360

Suma and Akashi

Ship	Builder	Laid down	Launched	Commissioned
Suma	Yokosuka NY	Aug 1892	Mar 9, 1895	Dec 1896
Akashi	Yokosuka NY	Aug 1894	Nov 1897	Mar 1899

The two ships of this class were of an orthodox design, but they were the first cruisers built entirely to a Japanese design and entirely by Japanese workers.

THE PROTECTED AND UNPROTECTED CRUISERS

1: *Hashidate*, the first armored cruiser built in Japan, is shown here. The ship was built to a French design and was already outdated by the Russo-Japanese War. The ship is dominated by the single 12.6in/40 gun mounted forward. The ungainly appearance was increased by the single stack amidships and the single mast fitted aft. The secondary battery and smaller guns were mounted in the hull.

2: This is *Chitose* in 1898. This compact and balanced ship had a powerful armament and good speed. Its appearance was dominated by two tall stacks and two masts. The ship had two single 8in guns fore and aft. The secondary battery of ten 4.7in guns was mounted singly along the hull.

3: This is the Japanese-built unprotected cruiser *Miyako* in 1905. The ship was lightly armed and was used as a dispatch ship and scout. The ship was fitted with two single 4.7in gun mounts and ten 47mm guns, most fitted in hull casemates.

1

2

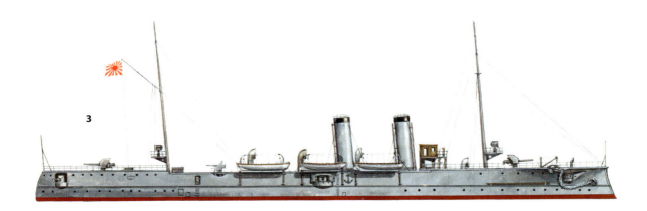

3

Akashi, seen here in 1899, was the first cruiser built in Japan to a Japanese design. Her single 6in forward gun and three starboard beam 4.7in guns are evident in this view. This useful ship saw action throughout the war from Chemulpo to Tsushima. (Yamato Museum).

Upon completion *Suma* was found to have stability issues which required that *Akashi* be modified with a flush deck and no fighting tops. *Akashi* saw action at the battle of Chemulpo and both were present at Yellow Sea. On December 10, 1904 *Akashi* was mined, but survived. Both ships were present at Tsushima.

Suma and *Akashi* Specifications

Displacement	*Suma* 2,657 tons normal; *Akashi* 2,756 tons normal
Dimensions	Length: *Suma* 306ft 9in, *Akashi* 295ft 3in; beam: *Suma* 40ft, *Akashi* 41ft 9in; draft: *Suma* 15ft 3in, *Akashi* 15ft 9in
Propulsion	Eight boilers producing 8,500 IHP
Speed	20kts
Range	1,200nm at 10kts
Protection	Armored deck 2in on the ends, 1in on flat section; gun shields 4.5in
Armament	two 6in/40, six 4.7in/40, ten 47mm, four 42mm, two 14in TT above waterline
Crew	310

Idzumi

Ship	Builder	Laid down	Launched	Commissioned
Idzumi	Armstrong	Apr 5, 1881	Jun 6, 1883	1884

Idzumi is seen here in March 1905 just before the battle of Tsushima, during which she proved valuable as a scout. The cruiser missed the war against the Chinese, but served capably in the war against the Russians. By 1904, she had been re-armed with two single 6in guns fore and aft and three 4.7in guns on each beam. (Yamato Museum)

This Armstrong-built ship was the prototype of the firm's protected cruisers built for export. The ship had a heavy armament for her size and was the first to have the arched armored deck cover from side to side. The ship was originally built for Chile, but the Japanese sought to purchase her as the Sino-Japanese War approached. The ship was acquired via Ecuador, but did not enter service in time for the war. After being re-armed with smaller guns to address stability problems, *Idzumi* did see considerable action in the Russo-Japanese War. She was present at Yellow Sea, and at Tsushima she was among the first to sight the approaching Russian fleet.

Idzumi (1902) Specifications

Displacement	2,800 tons normal
Dimensions	Length 270ft; beam 42ft; draft 18ft 3in
Propulsion	Four boilers producing 6,500 IHP
Speed	18.25kts
Range	2,200nm at 10kts
Protection	Armored deck 3in on the ends, 1in on flat section; gun shields 2.25in; conning tower 2in
Armament	two 6in/40, six 4.7in/40, two 57mm, six 47mm, three 18in TT above waterline
Crew	300

Takasago

Ship	Builder	Laid down	Launched	Commissioned
Takasago	Armstrong	Apr 1896	May 18, 1897	May 1898

Takasago was another British-built cruiser which possessed a fine blend of speed, protection and firepower. The armament was entirely quick-firing. The single, heavy 8in guns fitted forward and aft made the ship lively in heavy seas, so the fighting tops were placed low on the fore and mainmast to avoid further stability problems. The ship was well protected and had 109 watertight compartments and a double bottom with 18 compartments. The ship was active during the war against the Russians and saw action at the battle of the Yellow Sea. _Takasago_ was vulnerable to underwater damage, as were all cruisers of the day, and she was sunk by a mine on the night of December 12/13, 1904 some 37 miles south of Port Arthur with a loss of 274 of her crew.

Protected cruiser _Takasago_ in May 1898. Her main armament of two single 8in guns is evident, as is the secondary battery of 4.7in and 3in guns placed along the main deck. The cruiser was lost in the war to a mine. (_Ships of the World Magazine_)

Takasago Specifications

Displacement	4,160 tons normal; 5,260 tons full load
Dimensions	Length 387ft overall; beam 46ft 6in; draft 20ft 6in (full load)
Propulsion	Eight boilers producing 15,500 IHP
Speed	23.5kts (design); achieved 22.9kts on trials
Range	5,500nm at 10kts
Protection	Armored deck 4.5in on ends, 2.5in on flat section; gun shields 4.5in to 2.5in; 4.5in conning tower
Armament	two 8in/40, ten 4.7in/40, twelve 3in/40, six 47mm, five 18in TT above waterline
Crew	425

Kasagi Class

Ship	Builder	Laid down	Launched	Commissioned
Kasagi	Cramp (Philadelphia)	Mar 1897	Jan 20, 1899	Nov 1899
Chitose	Union Iron Works (San Francisco)	May 1897	Jan 23, 1898	Mar 1899

These were the first warships purchased from the United States since 1865 and were ordered as gratitude for American neutrality in the Sino-Japanese War. In appearance and capabilities they were equivalent to the British-built _Takasago_. The ships were fitted with an identical gun armament and had one less torpedo tube with the deletion of the bow tube. The displacement of

This 1899 photograph shows *Kasagi*, lead ship of an American-built class of two protected cruisers. The main battery of two single 8in guns is evident, as are the numerous secondary guns. (Yamato Museum)

these ships was greater, but this was made up for by the increased power of the machinery. Both ships were present at the Yellow Sea where *Chitose* conducted a chase of Russian cruiser *Novik*. At Tsushima, both ships were heavily engaged and both were lightly damaged.

Kasagi and *Chitose* Specifications

Displacement	*Kasagi* 4,900 tons normal, *Chitose* 4,760 tons normal; *Kasagi* 6,066 tons full load, *Chitose* 5,598 tons full load
Dimensions	Length: *Kasagi* 402ft overall, *Chitose* 396ft; beam: *Kasagi* 48ft 9in, *Chitose* 49ft 3in; draft: *Kasagi* 20ft 9in, *Chitose* 20ft (full load)
Propulsion	Twelve boilers producing 15,000 IHP
Speed	22.7kts (*Chitose* 22.9kts)
Range	*Kasagi* 4,200nm at 11.5kts, *Chitose* 4,500 at 11kts
Protection	Armored deck 4.5in on ends, 2.5in on flat section; gun shields 4.5in to 2.5in; 4.5in conning tower
Armament	two 8in/40, ten 4.7in/40, twelve 3in/40, six 47mm, four 18in TT above waterline
Crew	*Kasagi* 405, *Chitose* 434

Tsushima and *Niitaka*

Ship	Builder	Laid down	Launched	Commissioned
Tsushima	Kure NY	Oct 1, 1901	Dec 15, 1902	Feb 14, 1904
Niitaka	Yokosuka NY	Jan 7, 1902	Nov 15, 1902	Jan 27, 1904

The largest Japanese-built protected cruisers to see action during the war were the two ships of the Tsushima class. *Niitaka*, seen here just after the war in 1906, entered service in 1904 just in time to engage the Russians at Chemulpo. (Yamato Museum)

After a gap of nine years, the IJN laid down another class of protected cruisers built to a Japanese design. These were heavily armed ships for their size and proved successful in service. *Tsushima* was present at both the battles of the Yellow Sea and Tsushima. *Niitaka* was in action at Chemulpo on the first day of the war and also saw action at Tsushima.

Tsushima and Niitaka Specifications

Displacement	3,366 tons normal; 3,716 tons full load
Dimensions	Length 339ft; beam 44ft 1in; draft 16ft 1in
Propulsion	Sixteen boilers producing 9,500 IHP
Speed	20kts
Range	4,000nm at 10kts
Protection	Armored deck 2.5in on ends, 1.5in on flat section; 4in conning tower
Armament	six 6in/40, ten 3in/40, four 47mm
Crew	320

Otowa

Ship	Builder	Laid down	Launched	Commissioned
Otowa	Yokosuka NY	Jan 3, 1903	Nov 2, 1903	Sep 6, 1904

Otowa was a smaller and faster version of the two previous protected cruisers built in Japanese yards. She was completed during the war, and saw action at Tsushima where she assisted in the sinking of a Russian cruiser.

Entering service during the war, the Japanese-built *Otowa* was heavily armed for her size with two single 6in guns and 4.7in and 3in guns along the hull. (Yamato Museum)

Otowa Specifications

Displacement	3,000 tons normal; 3,388 tons full load
Dimensions	Length 341ft (overall); beam 41ft 5in; draft 15ft 11in
Propulsion	Ten boilers producing 10,000 IHP
Speed	21kts
Range	7,000nm at 10kts
Protection	Armored deck 3in on ends, 2in on flat section; gun shields 1.5in; conning tower 4in
Armament	two 6in/50, six 4.7in/40, four 3in/40, two 18in TT above waterline
Crew	320

Unprotected Cruisers, Coastal Defense Ships, and Gunboats

A number of older ships, dating back as far as 1880, were still in service and were active during the Russo-Japanese War. Since they were too slow or too unprotected to operate with the fleet, they were assigned duties such as the coastal defense of Japan or escorting transports to and from Korea. Some ships also directly supported the ground operations of the Imperial Army. The most useful of these ships were the four cruisers used as scouts and dispatch ships. Several old armored ships built in the 1880s are detailed in most accounts as cruisers, but were actually considered by the IJN as coastal defense ships. These are included here under that category since this better depicts their capabilities and how they were used by the IJN.

Chihaya was representative of the small cruiser-sized ships used by the IJN in a variety of roles. The ship was unarmored but possessed good speed and two 4.7in guns. (*Ships of the World* Magazine)

Cruisers

Name	Built	Year in Service	Displacement (tons)	Dimensions (ft, length/beam/draft)	Speed (kts)	Armament	Remarks
Yaeyama	Yokosuka NY	1892	1,584 (normal)	318x35x13 (all rounded up)	21	three 4.7in eight 47mm two 18in TT	
Miyako	Kure NY	1890	1,772 (normal)	315x34x14	20	two 4.7in/40 ten 47mm two 15in TT	Mined and sunk May 14, 1904 northeast of Port Arthur
Chihaya	Yokosuka NY	1901	1,464 (full load)	288x32x10	21	two 4.7in/40 four 3in five 18in TT	
Tatsuta	Armstrong	1894	830 (normal)	240x28x10	21	two 4.7in four 47mm five 37mm five 15in TT	Originally built as a torpedo cruiser; ran aground on May 15, 1904 but repaired by Aug 30

Coastal Defense Ships

Name	Built	Year in Service	Displacement (tons)	Dimensions (ft, length/beam/draft)	Speed (kts)	Armament	Remarks
Kaimon	Yokosuka NY	1884	1,429 (full load)	211x33x16 (all rounded up)	12	one 6.7in six 4.7in one 3in	Wooden construction; sunk by mines on Jul 5, 1904
Tenryu	Yokosuka NY	1885	1,525 (normal)	210x36x17	12	one 6.7in six 4.7in one 3in	Wooden construction
Sai-yen	Vulcan (Stettin)	1885	2,440 (normal)	246x35x15	15	two 8.3in/35 one 5.9in/35 eight 47mm four 18in TT	Captured from China in Feb 1895; mined west of Port Arthur, Nov 30, 1904
Katsuragi	Yokosuka NY	1887	1,478 (normal)	207x35x15	13	two 6.7in five 4.7in eight 47mm two 15in TT	Composite construction
Yamato	Yokosuka NY	1887	1,478 (normal)	207x35x15	13	two 6.7in five 4.7in eight 47mm two 15in TT	Composite construction
Musashi	Onohama (Kobe)	1888	1,478 (normal)	207x35x15	13	two 6.7in five 4.7in eight 47mm two 15in TT	Composite construction
Takao	Yokosuka NY	1889	1,927 (full load)	233x35x13	15	four 6in two 47mm two 18in TT	Built to a French design; modernized in 1900

Gunboats

Name	Built	Year in Service	Displacement (tons)	Dimensions (ft, length/beam/draft)	Speed (kts)	Armament	Remarks
Banjo	Yokosuka NY	1880	708 (full load)	153x26x13 (all rounded up)	10	one 8.3in/22 one 4.7in/25 two 3.1in	
Tsukushi	Armstrong	1883	1,542 (full load)	210x32x18	16	two 10in four 4.7in one 3in two 47mm two 18in TT	Bought from Chile as a protected cruiser; reclassified as a gunboat in 1898
Maya	Onohama (Kobe)	1887	612 (normal)	154x27x10	12	two 6in/22 two 57mm	Iron hull
Chokai	Ishikawajima (Tokyo)	1888	612 (normal)	154x27x10	12	one 8.3in/22 one 4.7in/25	Iron hull
Atago	Yokosuka NY	1889	612 (normal)	154x27x10	12	one 8.3in/22 one 4.7in/25	Composite wood and iron hull; lost by accident southwest of Port Arthur, Nov 6, 1904
Akagi	Onohama (Kobe)	1890	612 (normal)	154x27x10	12	four 4.7in/40 six 47mm	Steel hulled
Heien	Foochow Dockyard	1890	2,640 (full load)	230x40x14	10	one 10.2in two 6in/40 eight 3in four 18in TT	Built in China to German plans; captured February 1895; mined west of Port Arthur, Sep 18, 1904
Oshima	Onohama (Kobe)	1892	630 (normal)	176x26x9	16	four 4.7in/40 five 47mm	Sunk in collision with *Akagi* northeast of Port Arthur, May 17, 1904
Uji	Kure NY	1903	620 (normal)	189x27x7	12	three 3in/40	

Musashi, seen here in 1897, was of little use by the time the IJN went to war with Russia. Having slow-firing breech-loading guns, little speed and no protection, this antiquated ship was assigned to coastal defense. (*Ships of the World* Magazine)

Akagi, seen here in 1897, was representative of the small gunboats used by the IJN to operate in support of the Imperial Army. Her main battery consisted of two 4.7in single guns. (*Ships of the World* Magazine)

The first destroyers built in Japan were the Harusame class. These ships were based on the design of the Shirakumo class. The ships incorporated the modified gun configuration which included the 3in mount forward, as can be seen in this 1905 view. (*Ships of the World* Magazine)

Destroyers and Torpedo Boats

One of the most promising naval technologies of the late 19th century was the self-propelled torpedo. This technology was especially appealing to the IJN as it searched for ways to counter stronger opponents. As an upstart navy, the IJN went through a period of favor with the French *Jeune Ecole* (Young School) which espoused that battleships were too expensive and vulnerable because they could be countered by inexpensive and powerful ships carrying torpedoes. This theory seemed very promising since the torpedo had advanced from a primitive and erratic weapon upon its invention in 1866 to the point in the 1890s where it was fairly reliable and could reach speeds of 30 knots.

A new type of naval unit was invented to carry the torpedo, and this was named the torpedo boat. These were small craft with a short range that were unable to operate in rough seas. They carried only a small number of torpedoes, but since battleships carried no dedicated anti-torpedo defenses, torpedoes boats were embraced by all the major naval powers, including the IJN. The IJN saw them as a useful weapon in the Yellow Sea or in coastal waters off Korea where the Japanese expected the war against the Russians to be fought. Most of the first IJN torpedo boats were bought from France, since the French were the primary proponent of these craft. The IJN also ordered torpedo boats from the Germans and even the British. Since these were fairly simple craft to build, construction was soon transferred to Japan.

The torpedo boat threat prompted a search for ways to counter it. Battleships were fitted with large numbers of quick-firing guns for defense, and torpedo nets were also fitted but these were only suitable when anchored or when the ship was moving at slow speeds. The best method to counter the torpedo boat was to build a bigger and better-armed torpedo boat which had the speed to chase them down and the firepower to destroy them. This resulted in what was called the torpedo boat destroyer, later simply referred to as a destroyer. Since the Royal Navy placed a great priority on negating the torpedo boat threat, the British built the first and best destroyers of the period. The first IJN destroyers were built in Britain, but construction was fairly quickly transferred to Japan.

G

THE DESTROYERS AND TORPEDO BOATS

1: This depicts the British-built destroyer *Akebono* in a dark-gray scheme. The ship's main armament was two 18in single trainable torpedo tubes fitted aft. A 3in gun was mounted aft to counter torpedo boats. Another was placed forward, as shown here, due to war experience. Four small stacks service the four boilers which created power to drive the ship at a maximum speed of 31 knots.

2: This depicts the British-built destroyer *Shiranui*. Built by the firm of Thornycroft, the ship had a different appearance than the *Akebono* above. The two 18in torpedo tubes are evident as is the 3in gun aft and the five 57mm guns, three of which were mounted around the forward superstructure. Only two stacks were needed to service the three boilers.

3: This shows torpedo boat *Hayabusa* in 1905. She was the lead ship in the large class of torpedo boats built to a French design. Two of the boat's three torpedo tubes are visible in this profile as is the light gun battery.

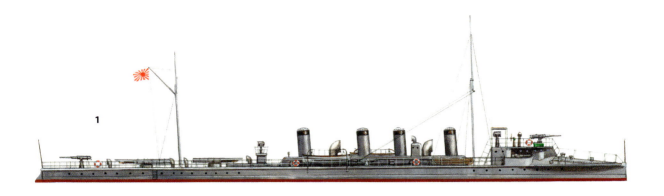

1

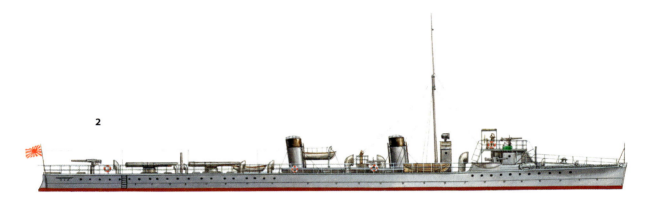

2

3

ABOVE *Sazanami*, shown here in 1900, was a member of the six-ship Ikazuchi class. Two single 18in torpedo tubes can be seen aft; a single 3in gun was also fitted aft. The ship also carried 5 57mm single guns fitted forward and amidships to attack torpedo boats. (*Ships of the World* Magazine)

RIGHT The six-ship Murakumo class was also built in Britain and shared a similar layout to the Ikazuchi class. This is the lead ship of the class in 1900. (*Ships of the World* Magazine)

The destroyer became a signature weapon of the IJN. It carried both torpedoes and guns, and with its high speed and greater endurance, was well-suited for both defending the IJN's battle fleet and attacking the enemy's. The lure of a small ship crewed by a brave and well-trained crew able to direct great blows at the enemy's most powerful ships was irresistible to the Japanese leading up to the Russo-Japanese War and for the remainder of the IJN's existence.

The war record of the IJN's destroyers was mixed. Even the success in the opening attack of the war, the night torpedo attack against the surprised and partially illuminated Russian fleet anchored off Port Arthur in the night of February 8/9 when three hits were scored on Russian ships, has to be seen as an overall disappointment in view of the very favorable tactical situation present for a torpedo attack. For the remainder of the Port Arthur campaign, including the battle of the Yellow Sea, the performance of the IJN's destroyers was dismal with not a single torpedo hit being recorded. This lack of success was attributed to faulty tactics which stressed long-range fire. After the IJN altered its torpedo tactics, the results did improve. At Tsushima, 20 destroyers engaged in torpedo attacks, firing a total of 24 torpedoes and scoring a total of three hits on two different Russian battleships.

Destroyers

Name	Builder	Year in Service	Displacement (tons)	Dimensions (ft, length/beam/draft)	Speed (kts)	Armament	Remarks
Murakumo (lead ship in class of six)	Thornycroft (Chiswick, London)	1898	361 (full load)	215x20x6 (all rounded up)	30	one 3in/40 five 57mm two 18in TT	
Kagero, *Shinonome*, *Shiranui*, and *Yugiri*	Thornycroft (Chiswick)	1899	361 (full load)	215x20x6	30	one 3in/40 five 57mm two 18in TT	
Usugumo	Thornycroft (Chiswick)	1900	361 (full load)	215x20x6	30	one 3in/40 five 57mm two 18in TT	
Ikazuchi (lead ship in class of six)	Yarrow (Poplar, London)	1899	410 (full load)	225x21x5	31	one 3in/40 five 57mm two 18in TT	
Inadzuma, *Akebono*, *Sazanami*, and *Oboro*	Yarrow (Poplar)	1899	410 (full load)	225x21x5	31	one 3in/40 five 57mm two 18in TT	

Niji	Yarrow (Poplar)	1900	410 (full load)	225x21x5	31	one 3in/40 five 57mm two 18in TT	
Shirakumo and *Asashio*	Thornycroft (Chiswick)	1902	428 (full load)	223x21x6	31	one 3in/40 five 57mm two 18in TT	Enlarged Murakumo class with one extra boiler
Akatsuki	Yarrow (Poplar)	1901	415 (full load)	225x21x6	31	two 3in/40 four 57mm two 18in TT	Improved Ikazuchi class; mined and sunk near Port Arthur, May 15, 1904
Kasumi	Yarrow (Poplar)	1902	415 (full load)	225x21x6	31	two 3in/40 four 57mm two 18in TT	Improved Ikazuchi class; torpedoed Russian cruiser *Pallada*, Feb 9, 1904
Harusame (first of class of seven)	Yokosuka NY	1903	435 (full load)	234x22x6	29	two 3in/40 four 57mm two 18in TT	Japanese version of Shirakumo class; badly damaged by Russian gunfire at Tsushima, May 27, 1905
Hayatori	Yokosuka NY	1903	435 (full load)	234x22x6	29	two 3in/40 four 57mm two 18in TT	Mined and sunk near Port Arthur, Sep 3, 1904
Murasame and *Asagiri*	Yokosuka NY	1903	435 (full load)	234x22x6	29	two 3in/40 four 57mm two 18in TT	
Fubuki	Kure NY	Feb 1905	435 (full load)	234x22x6	29	two 3in/40 four 57mm two 18in TT	
Ariake	Kure NY	Mar 1905	435 (full load)	234x22x6	29	two 3in/40 four 57mm two 18in TT	
Arare	Kure NY	May 1905	435 (full load)	234x22x6	29	two 3in/40 four 57mm two 18in TT	

The two-ship Shirakumo class was an enlarged Murakumo design with slightly greater speed but it retained the same armament. This is *Asashio* in 1902. (*Ships of the World* Magazine)

Torpedo Boats

The IJN divided its torpedo boats into three types. First-class torpedo boats were greater than 120 tons displacement. These were given names, unlike the smaller boats which were given only numbers. Second-class boats displaced between 70 and 120 tons, and third-class boats less than 70 tons.

Early IJN torpedo boats were fragile craft and thus could only operate in favorable sea conditions and possessed a marginal speed advantage over the ships they were built to attack. Most of the early French-built or -designed torpedo boats, like Torpedo Boats *12*, *13*, *17*, *24*, and *26* shown here, were obsolescent before the war and were relegated to coastal defense duties. (*Ships of the World* Magazine)

Torpedo boats were used extensively during the Port Arthur campaign with boats from 11 different divisions seeing action. No boat older than the Torpedo Boat 31–38 class was used off Port Arthur. Those older and smaller boats were restricted to coastal and harbor defense in Japan during the war and saw no action.

At Tsushima, 28 torpedo boats from seven different divisions saw action. These boats scored five torpedo hits on four different Russian ships (three battleships and an armored cruiser).

Name	Builder	Year in Service	Displacement (tons)	Dimensions (ft, length/beam/draft)	Speed (kts)	Armament	Remarks
5–14, 16–19	Schneider (Chalons-sur-Saone)	1892–1894	54	115x11x3 (all rounded up)	19	two 47mm two 14.2in TT	
15 and 20	Normand (Le Havre)	1893	53	112x12x3	20	two 47mm two 14.2in TT	
21	Normand (Le Havre)	1894	80	118x13x5	20.7	one 47mm three 14.2in TT	
24	Kure NY	1895	80	118x13x5	20.7	one 47mm three 14.2in TT	
22–25	Schichau (Elbing)	1895	85	128x16x4	19	two 47mm three 15in TT	TB *25* built by Onohama (Nagasaki) with imported parts
26	Vulcan (Stettin)	1894	66	111x13x4	13.8	two 37mm two 14in TT	Captured from the Chinese in 1895
27	Vulcan (Stettin)	1894	72	111x14x4	15.5	two 37mm two 14in TT	Captured from the Chinese in 1895
29–30	Normand (Le Havre)	1898	88	121x14x4	22.5	one 57mm three 14.2in TT	
31–38	Schichau (Elbing)	1899	89	128x16x4	24	two 47mm three 15in TT	TB *34* and *35* sunk by gunfire at Tsushima, May, 1905; TB *38* damaged off Port Arthur on Aug 11, 1904

39–43	Yarrow (Poplar)	1899	102	153x15x5	26	two 57mm three 14.2in TT	TB *42* sunk by Russian destroyer, Dec 15, 1904 following a night attack on a Russian battleship
44–49	Kawasaki (Kobe)	1900	89	128x16x4	24	two 47mm three 15in TT	Built to same design as TB *31–38*
50–59	*50–55* Yokosuka NY; *56–59* Kure NY	1900–1902	54	112x12x3	20	two 47mm two 14.2in TT	Improved version of TB *15*; TB *51* wrecked Jun 28, 1904; TB *53* mined off Port Arthur, Dec 14, 1904
60 and 61	Kawasaki (Kobe)	1901	89	128x16x4	24	two 47mm three 14.2in TT	Built to same design as TB *31–38*
62–66	Yarrow (Poplar)	1900	102	153x15x5	26	two 57mm three 14.2in TT	
67–75	*67–69* Yokosuka NY; *70–72* Sasebo NY; *73–75* Kawasaki (Kobe)	1901–1902	89	132x16x4	23.5	two 57mm three 14.2in TT	Built in Japan to a British design; TB *69* sunk at Tsushima
Kotaka	Yarrow (Poplar, London)	1886	203	165x19x6	19	four 37mm six 14.2in TT	Built in Britain; reassembled in Japan
Fukuryu	Krupp (Kiel)	1886	115	140x17x5	20	two 37mm four 15in TT	Captured from China in 1895
Shirataka	Schichau (Danzig)	1900	126	153x17x5	28	three 57mm three 17.7in TT	Built in Germany; reassembled in Japan
Hayabusa	Normand (Le Havre)	1899	152	148x16x5	28.5	one 57mm two 47mm three 17.7in TT	Built in France and reassembled in Japan
Kasasagi and Manazuru	Normand (Le Havre)	1900	152	148x16x5	28.5	one 57mm two 47mm three 17.7in TT	Built in France and reassembled in Japan
Chidori	Normand (Le Havre)	1901	152	148x16x5	28.5	one 57mm two 47mm three 17.7in TT	Built in France and reassembled in Japan
Aotaka, Kari, and Hato	Kure NY	1903	152	148x16x5	28.5	one 57mm two 47mm three 17.7in TT	Japanese copy of Hayabusa class
Hibari, Kiji, and Tsubame	Kure NY	1904	152	148x16x5	28.5	one 57mm two 47mm three 17.7in TT	Japanese copy of Hayabusa class
Hashitaka, Sagi, Kamone, Otori, and Uzura	Kawasaki (Kobe)	1904	152	148x16x5	28.5	one 57mm two 47mm three 17.7in TT	Japanese copy of Hayabusa class

Torpedo Boat *42*, pictured here, was typical of the boats which were active during the war. This unit was lost to Russian destroyers in December 1904. (*Ships of the World* Magazine)

CONCLUSION

The emerging IJN was challenged to make a number of choices from the technologies of the era. This was made easier as the IJN was not burdened with a large existing fleet or with an officer corps wedded to outdated ideas. The stakes for the success of the IJN were high, perhaps nothing less than national survival. The Japanese government poured a considerable percentage of the nation's economic resources into building a navy and, under the guidance of a far-sighted group of men led by Yamamoto Gombei, the IJN was successful beyond all expectations; by 1905 it had won two wars and risen to the front ranks of naval powers.

The quality of IJN ships which fought in the Russo-Japanese War was uniformly high. The main elements of the battle fleet, the six British-built battleships and the eight armored cruisers, were world class, and in many cases better than their foreign contemporaries. The technical capabilities of these ships were more than matched by the morale and exhaustive training of their crews; it was in this area that the Japanese far surpassed the Russians. However, the victorious IJN was not permitted to rest on its laurels. In the year following the end of the Russo-Japanese War, a new naval race began when the Royal Navy launched a new type of battleship that made all existing IJN battleships obsolete. Japan was forced to follow suit, and soon began to build a new battle fleet with the eventual goal of fighting the United States.

Significant numbers of torpedo boats were built in Japan. This is a representative example, Torpedo Boat *73*, with its two 57mm guns and two single torpedo tubes mounted amidships and aft. (*Ships of the World* Magazine)

BIBLIOGRAPHY

Corbett, Julian S., *Maritime Operations in the Russo-Japanese War, 1904–1905 (Volumes 1 and 2)*, Naval Institute Press, Annapolis, MD (2015)

Evans, David C., and Peattie, Mark R., *Kaigun*, Naval Institute Press, Annapolis, MD (1997)

Jentschura, Hansgeorg, Jung, Dieter, and Mickel, Peter, *Warships of the Imperial Japanese Navy, 1869–1945*, Naval Institute Press, Annapolis, MD (1977)

Olender, Piotr, *Russo-Japanese Naval War 1905 (Volume 1 Port Arthur)*, Stratus, Sandomierz, Poland (2009)

Olender, Piotr, *Russo-Japanese Naval War 1904–1905 (Volume 2 Battle of Tsushima)*, Stratus, Sandomierz, Poland (2010)

Watts, Anthony J., and Gordon, Brian G., *The Imperial Japanese Navy*, Macdonald, London (1971)

The largest class of IJN torpedo boats to see action during the war was the Hayabusa class of four ships assembled in Japan from French components. This is Hayabusa in 1900. Eleven more of this design were built in Japan. The ships carried two single torpedo tubes, one amidships and one aft, and a small battery of 57mm and 47mm guns. (Ships of the World Magazine)

INDEX

Page numbers in **bold** refer to illustrations and their captions